CONSERVATION AND YOU

NICHOLAS FAULKNER
AND JANEY LEVY

rosen publishing's
rosen
central®

New York

Published in 2019 by The Rosen Publishing Group, Inc.
29 East 21st Street, New York, NY 10010

Copyright © 2019 by The Rosen Publishing Group, Inc.

First Edition

All rights reserved. No part of this book may be reproduced in any form without permission in writing from the publisher, except by a reviewer.

Library of Congress Cataloging-in-Publication Data

Names: Faulkner, Nicholas, author. | Levy, Janey, author.
Title: Conservation and you / Nicholas Faulkner and Janey Levy.
Description: New York : Rosen Central, 2019 | Series: How our choices impact earth | Includes bibliographical references and index. | Audience: Grades 5–8.
Identifiers: LCCN 2017046736| ISBN 9781508181446 (library bound) | ISBN 9781508181453 (pbk.)
Subjects: LCSH: Environmentalism—Juvenile literature. | Conservation of natural resources—Juvenile literature.
Classification: LCC GE195.5 .F38 2019 | DDC 363.7—dc23
LC record available at https://lccn.loc.gov/2017046736

Manufactured in the United States of America

CONTENTS

INTRODUCTION

Today, the term "climate change" is in the news more than ever. What we hear less about, however, is conservation. Conservation is the act of taking care of and protecting our natural resources. It's about making careful decisions about our natural resources to avoid wasting or polluting them. And it's just as important as other aspects of planet-friendly living. Earth on the Edge reports that roughly 19.64 pounds (8.9 kilograms) of CO_2 is produced by burning a gallon of gasoline. The average American contributes about 18 tons (16.3 metric tons) of CO_2 per year, causing significant air pollution.

The good news is that there are many things we can do to preserve our natural resources. The easiest ones start in or near the home. Buying organic food is a good way to support sustainable farming practices. For food to be considered organic, it must be produced without chemical fertilizers and pesticides and be processed with only natural additives (such as those manufactured from soybeans, corn, or beets). But how do you know if a food is organic? For fresh fruits and vegetables, look at the price look-up (PLU) code, which is the code of numerals printed on the tiny sticker that is attached to the item. If it begins with 9, the fruit or vegetable is organic. For other food items—such as flour, pasta sauce, fruit juice, and prepared foods—read the label carefully. If it has the USDA (United States Department of Agriculture) organic seal, it's made with at least 95 percent organic ingredients. Foods that have at least 70 percent organic ingredients can use the claim "Made with Organic Ingredients."

It's easy to forget that most of the things we buy, especially plastics, eventually wind up in landfills, which we rarely see.

Another way to conserve is to simply consume less. Today, it's easier than ever to buy products online. Those goods pollute when they're being manufactured as well as when they're shipped to your home. On average, in the United States, everything we buy in just a year has a CO_2 footprint of about 2 tons (1.81 metric tons) per person. There's nothing wrong with buying the necessities. However, being more conscious of what you buy is taking a step in the right direction toward saving the planet.

You can also join the fight to protect the planet by teaming up with an environmental organization. For example, the Forest Stewardship Council (FSC) is a nonprofit, nongovernmental organization founded by loggers, foresters, environmentalists, and sociologists in 1993. Its goal is to promote the responsible, sustainable management of forests around the world. It sets standards that take into account the protection of forest watersheds, soil, and native species; restrictions on the use of chemicals; and fair-labor policies. It certifies companies whose practices meet its standards, and those companies are then entitled to put the FSC label on their products. When your family needs to buy wood products, including paper, look for the FSC label. It can help you choose sustainably produced goods.

We need to conserve the only Earth we have. Humans can't simply move to the planet next door if they make this one uninhabitable. Today, all of our natural resources, including the air, freshwater, soil, forests, oceans, and biodiversity, are at risk.

CHAPTER ONE

BIODIVERSITY AND CONSERVATION

The term "biodiversity" is popping up more and more lately. It literally means biological diversity, and it refers to the variety of species on Earth, the genes they contain, and the ecosystems they form. The variety of plants and animals you see in the forests, deserts, and oceans and all over the world is Earth's biodiversity. The reason why you might have heard this term more lately is because the world's species are under threat of extinction.

Maintaining biodiversity is a major concern of conservationists and environmentalists. Some people wonder, however, whether it's really that important. Does it matter if there are fewer frog or butterfly species? Such questions are really asking whether it matters *to humans* if there are fewer species. The answer is yes. Everything is interconnected. Humans are part of this web, although they often mistakenly think of themselves as outside of it. And changes in one part of it affect the whole. That idea may seem pretty abstract, but scientists identify several concrete reasons biodiversity is important.

Biodiversity plays a major role in the health of the world's ecosystems. Every species has a role in supporting others.

HUMANS NEED BIODIVERSITY

Although people often don't recognize it, humans depend on biodiversity every day. It provides what scientists call ecosystem services. That term describes many practical benefits people receive from Earth's diverse ecosystems. They provide clean air and water, create and maintain fertile soil, pollinate crops, break down waste, and recycle nutrients. To provide these services, though, the ecosystems must remain healthy, and since every organism in an ecosystem has a role to play, all organisms are important.

Biodiversity also furnishes humans with food and medicines. Scientists believe that many plants and animals we know little about may one day provide nutritious food and medicines to fight terrible diseases.

Biodiversity has economic benefits as well. According to conservationtools.org, biodiversity promotes medicinal plants and other pharmaceuticals, which can lower health care costs. Also, tourism relies on biodiversity, as well as the fishing and hunting industries, which amount to billions of dollars a year.

Finally, biodiversity provides natural beauty. If you've ever visited a state or national park, or even simply walked through an unspoiled natural area near your home, you've had a chance to enjoy the beauty of nature. For all these reasons, biodiversity is important. It's also in danger.

Many current human actions threaten biodiversity. As the human population grows, it requires increasing amounts of food.

Humans consume more and more of the planet's resources. Overhunting and overfishing push species to the edge of extinction. Humans create pollution that harms resources, and they build cities and clear land without adequate consideration of the environmental

Human development, such as growing suburbs and cities, can have a negative effect on the species that inhabit those spaces by destroying animal habitats and displacing species.

impacts. They destroy habitats. They introduce invasive species that upset the balance of ecosystems. They fuel global warming, which threatens to throw all of Earth's ecosystems out of balance. It's important for people to take action to protect Earth's biodiversity.

PROTECTING EARTH'S SPECIES

The list of things you can do to protect biodiversity is almost endless. That's because all the steps you take to

MEASURING BIODIVERSITY

It's one thing to say that humans are having a negative effect on biodiversity. But how can we tell from a scientific standpoint? Biodiversity is hard to measure. But scientists can do it in a number of ways.

They can do it by counting the number of species, measuring the types of species, or by measuring the inter-actions among species that affect their ecosystems. They then track how these factors change over time. However, at the time of this writing, it's not possible to measure bio-diversity with much accuracy because of a lack of enough scientific data.

One thing is clear, though. Species are growing extinct at an astounding rate. It's normal that about one to five species become extinct every year. However, scientists estimate that we're now losing dozens of species per day!

conserve air, water, soil, forests, and oceans also help biodiversity. Remember—everything is interconnected.

Reduce your carbon footprint. Choose green prod-ucts whenever you can. When you do have hazardous products, dispose of them properly to avoid creating pollution. Choose food and goods produced using sus-tainable, environmentally friendly methods. As much as possible, choose food and goods produced locally. Don't buy items that are made from endangered species

One way to reduce our carbon footprint is to harness energy from the sun. Using solar panels is a clean, green way to power our homes and vehicles.

or that threaten their habitats. Join a conservation organization. Write to government leaders. Let them know how important it is to maintain biodiversity. Urge them to pass laws that will help fight global warming. Urge them to protect forests, oceans, and wilderness areas.

The challenges threatening biodiversity are enormous, and the need to act is great. The difficulties can seem overwhelming, but remember—even little steps make a difference. Plant a tree to shade a house and keep it cool, and you may keep up to 2,000 pounds (900 kg) of carbon out of the atmosphere, according to the Nature Conservancy. So take that first step today, and encourage all your friends and family to take it with you. Working together, everyone can make wise choices about conservation and protect the planet!

CHAPTER TWO

BREATHE FREE: MAINTAINING CLEAN AIR

t's hard to imagine that with the size of the atmosphere, we have a lack of clean air. But there are now some cities where the air is so polluted, residents need to wear masks.

Air pollution results when waste—in the form of gases or particulates (tiny particles of matter)—dirties the air. Some pollutants are toxic. Others produce damage through changes they cause in Earth's atmosphere.

Some pollution comes from natural sources. Volcanic eruptions, for example, may send particulates and toxic sulfur oxides (sulfur-oxygen compounds) into the atmosphere. Microorganisms in the digestive systems of cows and in rice fields produce a gas called methane. However, most experts believe that human activities produce most air pollution.

Industrial processes generate numerous pollutants, including ammonia, hydrocarbons (organic hydrogen-carbon compounds), sulfur oxides, and particulates containing lead and other harmful metals. Industry's transportation and electricity demands also contribute heavily to air pollution. Of course, the transportation and electricity demands of ordinary people contribute substantially, too.

Transportation is the leading cause of air pollution in most industrialized countries, including the United States and Canada. It produces carbon monoxide (CO), CO_2, hydrocarbons, and nitrogen oxides (nitrogen-oxygen compounds). These last two pollutants react in the presence of sunlight to form ozone, the main ingredient in photochemical smog.

Electricity production contributes significantly to air pollution. Most electricity in the United States and Canada is produced by burning oil, coal, or natural gas, putting nitrogen oxides, sulfur oxides, CO_2, and particulates into the air in the process.

Motor vehicles are one of the worst polluters on the planet, emitting tons and tons of greenhouse gases into the atmosphere each year.

Numerous ordinary activities also pollute the air. Burning trash releases harmful particulates and toxins such as dioxins. Lighter fluid applied to charcoal in barbecue grills puts out harmful chemicals. Aerosol sprays send tiny droplets of the product into the air—and into your lungs. Filling your car with gasoline releases

HOW AIR POLLUTION HARMS US

So what are the consequences of all this air pollution? It harms living organisms, affects soil fertility, and even damages roads and buildings.

Air pollution worsens and sometimes causes asthma and other respiratory conditions. Particulates, ozone, sulfur dioxide (SO_2), and nitrogen oxides harm people's air passages and lungs. Carbon monoxide interferes with your blood's ability to deliver oxygen throughout your body. Some chemical compounds can cause cancer and birth defects.

Air pollutants hurt livestock and wild animals. They can damage or kill crops. They also harm forests. Nitrogen oxides and SO_2 can produce acid rain, which pollutes rivers and lakes and harms the animals and plants living in them. Acid rain can also reduce soil fertility. Air pollution damages human-made products. It harms plastics, rubber, and fabrics; dissolves concrete and stone; and causes metals to corrode more rapidly than usual.

Some air pollutants cause harm by altering Earth's atmosphere. Carbon dioxide, methane, and nitrous oxide (N_2O) are among the gases known as greenhouse gases. Just as a greenhouse's glass traps heat inside it, these gases trap the sun's heat on Earth. Naturally occurring greenhouse gases keep Earth warm enough to support life. However, human activities have significantly contributed to the greenhouse gas concentrations in the atmosphere and quite possibly could be causing Earth's overall temperature to rise.

This effect is known as global warming or climate change. So far, it has produced severe droughts, terrible wildfires, deadly heat waves, stronger hurricanes, and floods, and it has damaged coral reefs, alpine meadows, and other habitats around the world. Scientists are also discovering that there is a rapid melting of glaciers as well as Arctic and Antarctic ice. This melting threatens to raise ocean levels enough to cause severe coastal flooding and endanger polar bears, penguins, and other wildlife of these frozen regions. The situation is serious. Fortunately, there are actions each individual can take to help keep the air clean.

Major storms are an unintended consequence of air pollution. They are a result of an increase in average global temperatures.

vapors that contribute to the formation of ozone. Cigarette smoke releases ten times more particulates than diesel car exhaust, according to a study conducted by Giovanni Invernizzi. And research by Congrong He, Lidia Morawska, and Len Taplin shows that some common laser printers produce as many particulates as cigarettes!

WHAT YOU CAN DO

It requires conscious decisions and effort, but each person can help reduce air pollution by reducing his or her carbon footprint. Since transportation is the leading cause of air pollution, that's a good place to start. The EPA reports that cars, trucks, ships, trains, and planes produced 27 percent of greenhouse gas emissions in 2015.

So walk or ride your bicycle whenever you can. If you live in a place that has good public transportation, use it.

Sometimes using a car is necessary, so drivers should develop driving habits that save fuel. Combine errands instead of making lots of short trips. Avoid "jackrabbit" starts and excessive braking, which burn extra fuel. Drive the speed limit. Gasoline mileage decreases at speeds over 55 miles (88 km) per hour. Make sure your tires are properly inflated because low tire pressure reduces gasoline mileage. Refuel after dusk. That reduces the amount of ozone-causing fumes that escape. Be careful not to spill gasoline because the spilled fuel releases fumes. If your family plans to buy a new car, purchase the most fuel-efficient one that your family can afford.

There are still other ways to reduce gasoline usage. For example, buy local food and goods whenever possible. Because they haven't been transported great distances, they haven't required a lot of gasoline to get to you. Gasoline-powered lawn mowers contribute to air pollution. According to a report by Anders Christensen, Roger Westerholm, and Jacob Almén, running a gasoline-powered lawn mower for one hour creates about the same amount of air pollution as a 100-mile (161 km) car ride! So if your family has a gasoline-powered lawn mower, consider getting an old-fashioned reel mower.

Simple habits, such as turning off lights when not in use, can be a great way to conserve energy and maintain a greener home.

Because generating electricity produces substantial amounts of air pollution, reduce your electricity usage. Climb the stairs instead of using the elevator or escalator. Use compact fluorescent bulbs (CFLs) and dispose of them properly when they're exhausted (check your local recycling programs). Turn off lights and unplug electronics and appliances when they're not in use. Even when they're turned off, they still use some electricity when they're plugged in.

Use appliances efficiently. That is, wash full loads of clothes and run the dishwasher only when it's full. Set the thermostat lower in the winter and higher in the summer. Turn the temperature on your water heater down to 120°F (50°C) instead of 140°F (60°C). If your family is planning on buying new appliances, choose energy-efficient models. Weatherize your home to reduce the amount of heat it loses in winter or lets in during summer. In some places, electricity providers allow customers to choose electricity generated by renewable, nonpolluting sources. Do that if you have the option. And always reduce, recycle, and reuse. Taking those steps greatly reduces the amount of electricity used to produce goods and the amount of fuel needed to transport them.

There are other measures you can take, too. Avoid aerosols and other products that pollute the air. Don't smoke. Don't burn trash. Write to government leaders to urge them to create laws that protect clean air. And encourage everyone you know to help keep the air clean!

MYTHS & FACTS

Myth: People can protect themselves from high levels of particulate air pollution outside by simply staying indoors.
Fact: When particulate levels are high outdoors, they're high indoors, too. The only way to avoid exposure to dangerous levels of particulates is to keep particulate levels low.

Myth: Conserving water will force people to make major changes in their lifestyles.
Fact: Everyone can conserve a lot of water through simple changes in behavior that reduce waste.

Myth: Logging in national forests will protect them by preventing disastrous forest fires and diseases.
Fact: Fire is a natural part of a healthy forest ecosystem, so trying to completely suppress fires isn't desirable. However, commercial logging changes forest ecosystems in ways that result in more severe fires and more tree deaths from disease.

CHAPTER THREE

SAVE OUR SOIL

Many people don't think of soil as important to life. They see it as just the dirt beneath their feet. But it's not something to take for granted. It's one of Earth's most important resources and provides nutrients to much of life, including plants and the animals that eat those plants for survival.

Soil consists of minerals combined with organic matter. The minerals come from the weathering, or wearing away, of rocks. The organic matter, called humus, comes from decomposing, or rotting, plant and animal remains. Healthy, fertile soil contains not only minerals and humus but also bacteria, which break down the humus into the nutrients plants need.

Soil is constantly being formed, so you might think there is no need to worry about it. However, the process of soil formation is slow. It has taken thousands of years to form the thin layer of fertile soil that covers the land. Yet, human activities can destroy that essential layer of fertile soil in just a few years.

HOW HUMANS ARE HARMFUL

A leading problem in soil conservation is erosion. Generally, erosion happens gradually. Human practices have greatly increased the rate of soil erosion, though, threatening this precious resource.

Much erosion results from the removal of vegetation to clear land for construction. The plants that were removed protected the soil from the potentially damaging effects of wind and rain. Their roots held the soil in place. In addition, the plants absorbed some of the rainwater, so there was less to run off the land and carry soil away. Similar problems occur in places where the timber industry practices clear-cutting, which is the removal of all trees in an area.

Overgrazing also contributes to erosion. If ranchers allow herds to graze too long in an area, it reduces the amount of organic matter in the soil. As a result, the soil erodes easily.

Clearing land for farmland plays a role in erosion, too. You may think that is odd. After all, farmers grow crops on their land. Don't the crops help hold the soil in place in the same way wild plants do? Not necessarily. For one reason, crops don't grow in the fields year-round. In addition, some farming practices increase erosion. According to the Natural Resources Defense Council (NRDC), one-third of the topsoil in the United States has been lost as a result of modern industrialized farming practices. One culprit is tilling, or plowing.

Though modern farming provides an abundance of crops, it can also hurt the very soil that feeds us. This is why responsible farming is so important.

Before planting, the land must be prepared through tilling. Conventional tillage removes most of the crop residue, the plant matter left from the previous harvest. Since that residue helps prevent erosion, removing most of it increases erosion. To prevent the problem, some farmers practice conservation tillage, which leaves at least 30 percent of the residue on the field. The timing of tillage is also a factor. It's best to leave the residue on fields through winter, to prevent erosion from rain and melting snow in the spring. However, a wet spring can force a farmer to delay tilling and planting, resulting in a smaller crop yield. Therefore, some farmers till in the fall, after the harvest, leaving fields exposed to erosion in the spring.

The practice of planting the same crop in a field year after year can reduce soil fertility. Corn, wheat, and some other grain crops drain nitrogen, an essential nutrient, from the soil. Farmers can avoid the problem by practicing crop rotation, alternating the nitrogen-draining crop with crops such as alfalfa or soybeans, which add nitrogen to the soil.

Chemical pesticides and fertilizers—used by home gardeners as well as farmers—also harm the soil. The chemicals can reduce the ability of the soil's bacteria to break down the humus. The soil may become harder as a result, making it less able to absorb water and thus easier to erode. The chemicals cause other problems as well. They can be washed into rivers and lakes, polluting the waters, and have been linked to cancer and other health problems in humans.

DIRT IS AMAZING

You wouldn't realize it just from looking at the ground beneath your feet, but there's a whole other world in the soil. One tablespoon of soil has more organisms than all the people on Earth. This includes five thousand different types of bacteria in just one gram.

There are 10 tons (9.07 metric tons) of living matter in the top 6 inches (15.2 centimeters) of each acre of soil. And those earthworms you see crawling around? There are 1.4 million of them in an acre (0.4 hectares) of cropland. Don't underestimate their appetite either. They consume 15 tons (13.6 metric tons) of dry soil per acre each year.

Aside from what's living in there, soil is an essential part of our lives. A tenth of the world's carbon dioxide emissions, which promote global warming, are stored in the soil. We better take care of our dirt considering that it takes at least five hundred years for Mother Earth to produce just 1 inch (2.5 centimeters) of topsoil.

WHAT CAN YOU DO?

There are many measures that you and your family can take to help protect the soil. One, for example, is to buy local organic food. Buying organic helps the local economy and reduces air pollution because the food didn't have to be transported a great distance to reach you. Buying local also gives you a chance to find out what kind of tillage a farmer practices. Purchasing food from local farmers who practice conservation tillage is a good way to protect the soil, even if their produce doesn't qualify as organic.

Don't limit your organic buying to foods. Buy organic clothing. Organic cotton is grown without the use of damaging chemical pesticides and fertilizers, whereas conventionally grown cotton depends heavily on both. Hemp produces vastly more fiber than cotton, without the use of pesticides, and it also adds nitrogen to the soil.

Shopping at local farmers' markets is a great way to conserve both the fossil fuels and preservatives that would otherwise be used for long-distance shipping.

Buy organic personal-care products, too. In terms of household products, you may not be able to buy organic products, but you can choose products that don't contribute to soil pollution or erosion. For example, buy paper products with a high recycled paper content to reduce the number of trees destroyed. Avoid chemical pesticides.

If you have a garden at home, make it organic, and do your own composting to fertilize it.

Grow plants native to your area. They're adapted to grow in the existing soil conditions, without requiring

Composting is a great way to reuse leftover organic matter, such as banana peels, by turning it into fertilizer.

the addition of chemicals that could be harmful. Make sure you and your family do garden and yard planting in a way that helps prevent erosion. For example, you can plant a rain garden to capture runoff water and keep it from washing soil away. If you have a lawn, leave grass clippings on the lawn after mowing to enrich the soil. Walk around your yard in aerator sandals. The spikes on the bottom can help loosen the soil and are an effective way to kill some lawn pests.

If your family uses oil heat and stores fuel oil in an underground tank, there are precautions you must take to protect the environment. The tank could rust, resulting in leaks and contamination of the soil with fuel oil. If your family notices that you seem to be using more fuel, have the tank tested for leaks. In fact, it should be tested regularly so small problems can be detected before they become large ones. Know the local, county, and state regulations that apply to fuel oil storage tanks, and make sure your family's tank meets them. If you need to get a new tank, get one that's double walled and has a monitor.

And although you may be getting tired of reading this advice—reduce, recycle, and reuse! Those are some of the most effective steps you can take for all aspects of conservation. Finally, write to your government leaders about the problems caused by chemical fertilizers and pesticides, and urge them to make laws that encourage and support more environmentally friendly soil practices.

CHAPTER FOUR

BE A FRIEND TO THE FORESTS

So much of life on Earth would not exist without the forests. In addition to the plant life that makes the forests, countless species of animals call it their home. Forests are the most richly diverse ecosystems on Earth. Even today, scientists are discovering new species that live in the forests.

Unfortunately, forests are severely endangered. People have been cutting down forests for farmland and cities ever since agriculture began about eleven thousand years ago. According to the NRDC, forests once covered almost 50 percent of Earth's land, or about 18 billion acres (7 billion ha). According to the Worldwatch Institute, people have destroyed about 7.5 billion acres (3 billion ha). And deforestation continues today. Oakley Brooks reports in *Nature Conservancy* that an area roughly the size of New York State—about 32 million acres (13 million ha)—is destroyed annually. This loss matters because forests are important for many reasons.

THE IMPORTANCE OF FORESTS

The world's forests have many kinds of value. One is economic value. Wood from forests is used in building, for making furniture and other products, and as fuel for heating and cooking. It's also used to make paper and processed wood products, such as cellophane, some plastics, and even fibers like rayon, which is used in clothing. Besides wood, forests provide latex (which is used to make rubber), fruits, nuts, oils, waxes, and resins.

Forests also have medical value. Rain forests, for example, have yielded medicines to fight diseases such as malaria, glaucoma (an eye disease), and cancer. A muscle relaxant sometimes used in heart surgery also comes from a rain forest plant. Scientists believe rain forests may hold many more medicines yet to be discovered.

Cutting down on our use of paper products is a clear and easy way to conserve our precious forests.

Forests have environmental value as well. They absorb large amounts of rainwater, preventing the rapid runoff that can result in erosion and flooding, and keeping rivers clean by preventing soil and pollutants from getting washed into them. Forests help renew the atmosphere. During photosynthesis, they give off oxygen, which people and all other animals need to breathe. They also remove CO_2, one of the greenhouse gases, from the air.

Forests have cultural value. In some places, such as New Guinea, people have lived in forests for centuries and have developed cultures centered on the forest. Without the forests, these cultures break down.

Forests have recreational value. Every year, millions of people enjoy visiting forests and hiking, camping, or simply appreciating their beauty.

Forests also provide a crucial habitat for thousands of wildlife species, many of which can live nowhere else. Tropical rain forests, for example, are home to more than half the plant and animal species on Earth, although they cover only about 6 percent of the planet.

Andrew Downie reports that Brazil's Atlantic Forest, although greatly reduced from the millions of acres it once covered, is home to one thousand bird species and twenty-six primate species. Two hundred of the bird species and twenty-one of the primate species are found nowhere else.

Tropical rain forests play an important role in regulating Earth's climate. By absorbing the sun's light and heat, they help regulate temperatures not only in their immediate region but also around the world. By taking in and holding on to CO_2, they help prevent the

Tropical rain forests host some of the most exotic and varied species in the world. As they disappear, so do the plants and animals that depend on them.

buildup of this greenhouse gas in the air. When tropical rain forests are destroyed, their CO_2 is released back into the atmosphere. Scientists estimate that deforestation currently contributes about 15 percent of the world's CO_2 emissions—more than transportation contributes. So threats to forests threaten Earth's environment as a whole.

Deforestation for commercial logging and agriculture endangers forests today. So does air pollution, which leads to acid rain, as well as soil and water pollution. Fortunately, you and your family have the power to do something about it.

THREATS TO THE FORESTS

When we think of forests, we tend to forget that they are an essential part of life on Earth. There's not one species on the planet that isn't affected by them in one way or another. The rain forests house more species of plant and animal than any other habitat on land. One-fifth of all plant and animal life live in the Indonesian rain forest alone. Yet, humans clear an area of rain forest the size of a football field every two seconds.

Humans have a relationship with the forests as well. Look in your medicine cabinet and you'll find that one in four of your medicines there likely originated from rain forest plants. Yet, only 1 percent of rain forest plants have been studied for medicinal use. Think of the potential if the other 99 percent were explored. Forests also play a critical role in slowing climate change by converting carbon dioxide into oxygen.

The Boreal forest (or Taiga) runs across the northern United States and Canada, and also from Norway to northern Japan. It's the largest land habitat on Earth. Sadly, it's also the most vulnerable to climate change and the cutting down of its trees for human consumption.

BE FRIENDLY TO THE FORESTS

People buy wood and wood products for many reasons. Perhaps they need a new piece of furniture. Perhaps they're building a deck on their house or maybe even a whole new house. They can face a dizzying array of choices while shopping, and it can be hard to determine which choice is the most environmentally friendly. But there are actions each person can take to help ensure that the wood or wood product being purchased has been sustainably harvested.

Look for the logo of the Forest Stewardship Council (FSC). It certifies that the wood comes from a responsibly and sustainably managed forest. If you can't find wood or wood products certified by the FSC, ask where the wood comes from. Woods from some places—especially hardwoods—are harvested in unsustainable ways. Hardwoods, often sought after by consumers, pose particular problems because they grow much more slowly than softwoods. Woods harvested in unsustainable ways may also be harvested using forced labor. Among the woods associated with poor practices are big-leaf mahogany, African mahogany, Spanish cedar, Caribbean pine, rosewood, and teak. So avoid lumber and furniture made from those woods.

You can also help protect forests by buying products made with wood substitutes such as bamboo. Or consider salvaged or recycled wood. You may not think of wood as something that can be recycled, but it can be, and it's one way to conserve forests. Many people

You can find recycled paper products just about anywhere these days, especially shopping bags.

like the look of wood reclaimed from old barns, for example. You and your family may also be able to get doors and window frames from salvage companies.

Many trees are logged to make paper and paper products. So you can help protect forests by choosing paper products with recycled paper content.

The higher the recycled content, the greater the reduction in new trees harvested. This applies to notebooks, printer paper, napkins, toilet paper, paper towels, and any other paper products you use. You should also look for ways to reduce the amount of paper you use. Do you really need to print that email or that funny story you found online? How about using cloth napkins instead of paper napkins, or old cloths for cleaning rather than paper towels? Reuse paper, too. Instead of throwing out paper with printing or writing on only one side, save it to use as scrap paper.

There are other steps you can take to protect forests as well. If you're going camping and will need firewood, buy wood where you'll be camping rather than taking wood from home. Wood brought into an area from outside may carry invasive insects or diseases. After hiking in a forest, clean your shoes or boots to avoid the risk of spreading diseases from that forest to the next place you hike. Join campaigns to plant trees to restore damaged forests. Avoid contributing to air, water, and soil pollution, which harm forests. Write to government leaders to urge them to pass laws protecting forests. And educate your family and friends about the dangers forests face and ways they can protect forests.

CHAPTER FIVE

THE MIGHTY WATERWAYS

L ife cannot exist without water. Luckily for us, more than 70 percent of Earth's surface is covered in this essential substance. Inside living organisms, it carries nutrients to every cell and carries away waste products.

People—plus land plants and animals and those living in rivers and lakes—need freshwater to exist. Freshwater is more vital for your survival than food. You can live for weeks without food but only a couple of days without water. In spite of freshwater's importance, people endanger it through many of their actions.

WHAT GETS INTO THE WATERWAYS

Toxic industrial wastes. Untreated sewage. Chemical fertilizers and pesticides from farms. Perhaps you picture those scenes when you think about water pollution. But other dangers lurk in the products people use and the activities they perform every day.

Air pollution, which can result from numerous common activities, can cause acid rain. Acid rain harms rivers and lakes, killing fish and other wildlife.

Many common household and personal-care products contain toxic ingredients. These toxins get washed through drains, sinks, and toilets into rivers and lakes. They harm fish and wildlife and increase not only the cost of creating clean water but also the amount of pollution-generating energy needed to clean the water.

Phosphates in detergents and in lawn and garden fertilizers cause water pollution. They greatly

Since our rivers and lakes sustain entire ecosystems of their own, any pollutants that find their way into our waterways affect those species.

increase the growth of algae. When the algae die, their decay uses up the water's oxygen, killing other life in the water.

A chemical used to make freshwater safe to drink also causes damage. US and Canadian laws require the addition of chlorine to kill harmful bacteria. Unfortunately, chlorine also kills helpful bacteria and is highly toxic to fish. In people, it can cause allergic reactions and has been linked to heart disease and cancer.

People also waste water and thus must use more energy to produce more clean water and deliver it to homes, schools, and businesses. Increased energy usage leads to increased pollution that harms water. Fortunately, you have the power to make a difference.

WHAT YOU CAN DO TO REDUCE WATER POLLUTION

Each person can help reduce water pollution. For starters, don't pour hazardous household products down the sink drain or flush them down the toilet. Instead, dispose of them through your town's hazardous waste program. If your community doesn't have a program, ask for one.

In addition, never flush unwanted medicines down the toilet or wash them down the drain. Take them to a pharmacy for safe disposal (many states and drugstores do have disposal programs) or take them out of their containers and throw them in the trash. Many medicines are unable to be broken down into simpler substances by bacteria (that is, they are not biodegrad-able). They could pass through treatment plants and still be in recycled water that communities use.

Avoid detergents and other polluting household cleaners. Instead, use baking soda, vinegar, natural cit-rus products, and cornstarch as cleaning agents. Baking soda and citrus products clean sink, tubs, toilets, and showers, and they brighten laundry. Vinegar cuts grease and removes mildew. Cornstarch can be used to clean windows and to shampoo carpets and rugs.

Choose personal-care products that don't contain detergents or toxic ingredients. Look for organic or nat-ural products with plant-based ingredients. Not only will they help protect Earth's water, but also they'll be better for your health.

Buy clothing made from organic cotton or hemp. These fibers come from plants grown sustainably, without chemical fertilizers and pesticides. Some com-panies also offer clothing colored with environmentally friendly earth and plant dyes.

Buy paper products that haven't been bleached with chlorine. Look for products labeled TCF (totally chlorine-free) or PCF (processed chlorine-free).

Use natural fertilizers such as compost or manure on lawns and gardens. You may be able to buy these fertilizers locally. You can also do your own composting. There are composting canisters you can buy that store the material, speed up decomposition, and have acti-vated carbon filters that reduce or eliminate odors.

Reduce, recycle, and reuse in all areas of your life. Producing and transporting goods and food uses

Be a champion water protector. Recycle as much as possible and help pick up trash to prevent litter from ending up in our waterways.

energy and creates pollution that often winds up in lakes and rivers. The more people consume, the more pollution they create.

SOME PRACTICAL STEPS

Some simple changes in your behavior can save water. Start in the kitchen. Instead of wasting tap water waiting for it to get cold enough to drink, keep drinking water in the refrigerator. If you wash dishes by hand, don't leave the water running the whole time. If you have a dishwasher, don't rinse dirty dishes before loading them; just scrape them. Run the dishwasher only when it's full.

Avoid waste in the bathroom, too. Don't leave the water running while you and your family members brush your teeth or shave. Take shorter showers. According to Environment Canada, a person's ten-minute shower uses about 53 gallons (200 liters) of water. If you take a five-minute shower instead, you can save more than 185 gallons (700 liters) of water every week.

Fix leaks and drips. According to the Natural Resources Defense Council, a dripping faucet can waste 20 gallons (76 liters) of water each day. A leaking toilet can waste 200 gallons (757 liters)!

If you have a garden, grow only plants native to your area. They're adapted to thrive there without a lot

PUTTING WASTEWATER TO WORK

There are two kinds of wastewater that households produce: black water and gray water. Black water is what goes down the toilet and isn't reusable—some places also consider kitchen sink water to be black water because it usually contains organic matter. The other is gray water. Gray water is wastewater that can be reused, not for consumption necessarily, but in other ways, such as in the garden, for watering houseplants, and even in the toilet tank to flush. It's what goes down the drains of showers, bathroom sinks, and out of washing machines. Reusing this gray water in creative ways can actually help reduce the strain on local water supplies.

Effectively capturing gray water can be a big job that requires replumbing certain household pipes. But one easy way to do it is every time you run the water waiting for it to heat up, place a bucket under the faucet. Instead of that perfectly good water going down the drain, you can save it to reuse elsewhere.

of extra water. Sprinklers lose water to evaporation. Use a soaker hose instead. Collect rain in a barrel for watering your plants. A fine mesh screen can prevent mosquitoes from breeding in the water. However, make sure your community allows standing water. Some prohibit it completely because there's always a risk that disease-bearing mosquitoes may breed.

Your family may want to consider replacing older equipment with more energy-efficient models. Front-loading washing machines use only about one-third to one-fourth the amount of water a top-loading

It's both great fun and an educational experience to plant native species, which use less water than those from other areas.

washer does. However, they're also very expensive to buy and thus not a good option for everyone. If a front-loading washing machine isn't right for your family, consider a new energy-efficient top-loader. They can reduce water usage by up to one-half.

Older toilets use 3.5 gallons (13.3 liters) per flush. Newer ones use 1.6 gallons (6 liters) or less. Some toilets even have one flush button for solid waste and a second for liquid waste. They use 1.6 gallons to flush solid waste and only 0.8 gallon (3 liters) to flush liquid waste! If replacing an older toilet isn't possible, fill a 1-gallon (4 liters) plastic bottle with water and put it in the toilet tank. By taking up space, it reduces the amount of water in the tank and thus the amount used per flush.

Put low-flow aerators on sink faucets and show-erheads. They mix air with the water and reduce the amount of water used by about half.

These are only some of the ways to reduce your water usage. You can probably think of others. As the numbers show, even just a few changes can make a big difference. Spread the word—talk with your family and friends to let them know how easy it is to conserve water!

CHAPTER SIX

CARE FOR THE OCEANS

Since humans live on land, it's hard for us to appreciate the greatness of the oceans. They cover most of the earth's surface and are so deep that, as of 2017, we have explored only 5 percent of their realm. Most people also don't realize that the oceans drive weather and support all living organisms. Most scientists believe life on Earth began in the oceans about 3.5 billion years ago.

You may be thinking, fine, oceans cover most of Earth and hold most of Earth's water. But ocean water is salt water. People—and land animals in general—can't drink it. Crops and other land plants can't grow with it. And it's not as if we're running out of ocean water; there's plenty. So why worry about the oceans? Oceans provide many benefits both for people and for the planet as a whole. Without the oceans, there would be no life on Earth.

WHY THE OCEANS ARE ESSENTIAL

Hundreds of thousands of plant and animal species live in the world's oceans. Many others—penguins and sea otters are just two examples—depend on oceans for food. People depend on oceans for food, too. People harvest millions of tons of fish and shellfish every year. In some places, seafood is people's main source of protein. Many people eat ocean plants such as kelp, too.

A BIG LITTLE PROBLEM

The plastics we find littering our oceans aren't just empty soda bottles and used toothbrushes we see on the shoreline. A lot of ocean debris also consists of what are called microplastics, which are plastics that are less than five millimeters long, the size of a sesame seed. Microplastics actually make up most of the debris in our oceans and Great Lakes. They can break off larger plastics until they're ground down into smaller and smaller bits.

A big source of microplastics, however, are microbeads, tiny pieces of plastic found in beauty products, soaps, and toothpaste. You may notice a rough sensation when you run certain types of soap over your skin. These are the microbeads, which manufacturers say helps to exfoliate the skin. These particles pass through water filtration systems and into our lakes and oceans. They're consumed by marine life and pass through the food chain as well as release toxins.

The good news is that Congress banned manufacturers from producing microbeads starting in January 2017. That's a good start for cleaning up the giant "micro" problem.

Besides food, people obtain medicines from the oceans. Chemicals from marine organisms help fight cancer, viruses, and severe pain. Scientists believe marine organisms may provide many more medicines.

Ocean sediments are used in construction and to restore damaged beaches. They also contain useful minerals, such as magnesium, which is used in the manufacture of a range of products.

The oceans are sources of energy. Rich deposits of oil and gas lie beneath the ocean floor. You've probably seen pictures of the offshore wells used to draw out these resources. But did you know that the oceans themselves can provide energy? In some places, the rise and fall of tides is used to produce electricity.

Believe it or not, some coastal communities also get drinking water from the ocean. The salt is removed in a process called desalination, making the water fit for humans to drink, cook with, and use to water their crops.

Though the oceans are vast, they're extremely sensitive to pollutants. Even the slightest change in their chemistry can have drastic consequences.

In addition to these benefits, there's another very important one—the oceans play a major role in regulating Earth's climate. Water changes temperature much more slowly than the air. In summer, the oceans take in and store heat. In winter, they slowly release it. Ocean currents carry heat from tropical waters toward the poles. This keeps the tropics from getting too hot and warms the regions near the poles. Oceans also absorb and store CO_2, helping prevent the buildup of this greenhouse gas in the atmosphere. In spite of the enormous importance of the oceans, thoughtless human activities have endangered them.

MANY THREATS

Overfishing—capturing fish faster than they can reproduce—poses a major threat to the world's oceans. Modern technology has enabled commercial fishing operations to vastly increase their catch. As a result, fisheries around the world have collapsed. And the consequences extend beyond individual species. Overfishing changes entire marine ecosystems and affects local economies, leaving fishermen with no way to earn a living.

Commercial fishing practices also result in enormous amounts of bycatch—unwanted or unintentional catch. Millions of tons of fish, as well as sea turtles, marine mammals such as dolphins, and even seabirds, die as bycatch every year.

Fish practices that involve dragging nets across the ocean floor cause immense damage to fragile habitats. It can take centuries for those habitats to recover.

Nutrients from fertilizers and livestock manure often make their way from fields to rivers and then to oceans, where they have the same harmful effects they do in freshwater. They can cause algae overgrowths that create enormous dead zones by using up oxygen, damage fragile coral reefs, or—because of toxins—kill fish and marine mammals and sicken people.

Though commercial fishing offers an abundance of fish to eat at an affordable price, the consequences of irresponsible fishing are harm to the oceans and marine life.

Heavy coastal development also damages oceans. Runoff from storms carries pollutants such as motor oil, trash, fertilizers, and pesticides. Trash left on beaches often winds up in the ocean.

Numerous other human activities threaten oceans. Military sonar testing causes whales and other marine mammals to strand themselves on beaches. Noise and water pollution from ships and offshore drilling disrupts the migration routes, feeding, and mating of marine animals. Global warming and ocean acidification from too much CO_2 in the water damage coral reefs, harming the entire reef ecosystem. Ocean acidification also interferes with shellfish growth.

What can you do about these problems? There are several steps you and your family can take to protect the world's oceans.

YOU CAN HELP PROTECT THE OCEANS

Fighting pollution is an important part of ocean conservation, and there are numerous ways to do it. Many of the steps outlined earlier for combating freshwater and air pollution are also important for battling ocean pollution. That's because pollution in rivers and the air often makes its way into oceans. For example, when levels of the greenhouse gas CO_2 are high, the excess CO_2 dissolves into water on the ocean's surface, causing ocean acidification.

So work to reduce your carbon footprint. Cut back on how much electricity you use. Walk, ride your bicycle, or use public transportation instead of driving. Buy local, organic food. Less CO_2 goes into the air because the food hasn't been transported as far. Since it's been grown without chemical fertilizers or pesticides, it's not adding those pollutants to Earth's waters.

Avoid using chemical fertilizers or pesticides on home lawns and gardens as well. Planting native species helps, since they're adapted to grow in local conditions. Choose green household cleaners. Dispose of household hazardous wastes properly; don't

If we all cut our carbon emissions by walking or riding bikes, we will contribute to restoring the health of the oceans.

pour them down the drain or flush them down the toilet. Reduce your use of plastic items. These often wind up in oceans, where wildlife may become entangled in them or be harmed by mistaking them for food. If you visit a beach, don't leave trash behind. Dispose of it properly.

Ocean conservation involves other steps as well. Whether you're eating at home or dining out, choose seafood that's been caught or raised in a sustainable, environmentally friendly way. The Monterey Bay Aquarium offers a seafood guide that you can print from its website and carry with you to help you make informed choices. Don't buy jewelry or other items made from real coral. Write to government leaders about the importance of protecting coastal wetlands, which help filter pollutants from runoff and keep it from entering ocean waters. Also encourage government leaders to create protected underwater parks, just as protected national parks have been created on land. And talk with friends and family about the importance of ocean conservation.

TEN GREAT QUESTIONS
TO ASK YOUR SCIENCE TEACHER

1. Which causes less pollution: using paper towels or electric hand dryers in public restrooms?
2. When ocean water is desalinated to make drinking water for coastal communities, how does it affect the marine life in the area?
3. Was the immense strength of Hurricanes Harvey, Irma, Maria, and Jose in the summer of 2017 the result of climate change?
4. Is burning coal to produce electricity less polluting than burning oil?
5. Will melting glaciers change the oceans' salinity?
6. Would using trains instead of trucks to transport goods reduce the amount of CO_2 put into the atmosphere?
7. Why does underwater sonar cause marine mammals to beach themselves?
8. Do forests speed up or slow down global warming?
9. What is "global dimming" and what does it have to do with air pollution?
10. Can offshore drilling and drilling in environmentally sensitive areas for oil and natural gas be done without causing environmental damage?

GLOSSARY

additive A substance added to something else, such as food, to affect a property, such as texture, color, or flavor.

aerator A device for mixing air into something.

bacteria Tiny living organisms that cannot be seen with the eye alone. Some bacteria cause illness or rotting, but others are helpful.

carbon footprint A measure of the impact human activities have on the environment in terms of the amount of greenhouse gases produced, measured in units of carbon dioxide.

chlorine A gas that is used in bleach and to purify water.

compost Decayed organic matter, such as leftover food, that is used as fertilizer.

corrode To wear away a little at a time.

dioxin A highly poisonous hydrocarbon compound that is formed as a result of combustion processes, including burning trash and fuels such as wood and coal.

emission A substance put into the air by industry, automobiles, and various human activities.

endanger To put in danger or at risk.

erosion The wearing away of land over time.

extinction The state of no longer existing.

fishery A place for catching fish or other marine animals.

invasive Describing an organism introduced into an area from outside and causing harm by spreading.

pesticide A poison used to kill pests.

phosphate A compound containing phosphorus that is used in fertilizers and some detergents.

photochemical smog Air pollution that results from a chemical reaction caused by sunlight.

photosynthesis The way in which green plants make their own food from sunlight, water, and a gas called carbon dioxide.

pollinate To spread pollen from one plant to another so that the plants can reproduce.

salvage To recover from rubbish as valuable or useful.

sediment Gravel, sand, or mud carried by wind or water.

sustainable Capable of being continued or maintained with little long-term effect on the environment.

toxin A poisonous substance, especially one that is produced by a living organism.

watershed A region where water drains into a water supply such as a river or lake.

weatherize To make something, such as a house, better protected against winter weather.

FOR MORE INFORMATION

Conservation International
2011 Crystal Drive, Suite 500
Arlington, VA 22202
(800) 429-5660
Website: http://www.conservation.org
Conservation International's mission is to conserve
    Earth's living heritage—its global biodiversity—and
    to demonstrate that human societies are able to live
    harmoniously with nature.

Environment and Climate Change Canada
Public Inquiries Centre
7th floor, Fontaine Building
200 Sacré-Coeur Boulevard
Gatineau, QC K1A 0H3
Canada
(800) 668-6767 (in Canada only)
(819) 938-3860
Website: http://www.ec.gc.ca
Environment Canada's mission is to preserve and
    enhance the quality of Canada's natural environ-
    ment.

Greenpeace
702 H Street NW, Suite 300
Washington, DC 20001
(800) 722-6995
Website: http://www.greenpeace.org
Greenpeace works to organize peaceful protest and
    communication to educate the public about environ-
    mental problems and promote solutions.

Natural Resources Defense Council (NRDC)
40 West 20th Street, 11th Floor
New York, NY 10011
(212) 727-2700
Website: http://www.nrdc.org
Founded in 1970, the NRDC uses law and science to
    protect the planet's wildlife and wild places and
    to ensure a safe and healthy environment for all
    living things.

The Nature Conservancy
4245 North Fairfax Drive, Suite 100
Arlington, VA 22203-1606
(703) 841-5300
Website: http://www.nature.org
Founded in 1951, the Nature Conservancy works
    around the world to protect ecologically important
    lands and waters for nature and people.

FOR FURTHER READING

Gore, Albert. *Our Choice*. New York, NY: St. Martin's Press, 2009.

Grinspoon, David. *Earth in Human Hands: Shaping Our Planet's Future*. New York, NY: Grand Central, 2016.

Hawken, Paul. *Drawdown: The Most Comprehensive Plan Ever Proposed to Reverse Global Warming*. New York, NY: Penguin Books, 2017.

Horn, Miriam. *Rancher, Farmer, Fisherman: Conservation Heroes of the American Heartland*. New York, NY: W. W. Norton, 2017.

Kolbert, Elizabeth. *The Sixth Extinction: An Unnatural History*. New York, NY: Picador, 2015.

Mcdonald, Robert I. *Conservation for Cities: How to Plan and Build Natural Infrastructure*. Washington, DC: Island Press, 2015.

Moss, Stephen. *Planet Earth II*. London, UK: BBC Books, 2016.

O'Conner, Maura R. *Resurrection Science*. New York, NY: Palgrave Macmillan, 2015.

Robinson, Lori. *Saving Wild: Inspiration From 50 Leading Conservationists*. Los Angeles, CA: New Insights Press, 2016.

Taylor, Dorceta E. *Rise of the American Conservation Movement: Power, Privilege, and Environmental Protection*. Durham, NC: Duke University Press, 2016.

Wilson, Edward O. *Half-Earth: Our Planets Fight for Life*. New York, NY: Liveright Publishing Corporation, 2017.

BIBLIOGRAPHY

Audubon. "10 Incredible Facts About Dirt."
April 13, 2016. http://www.audubon.org/news
/10-incredible-facts-about-dirt.

Brooks, Oakley. "Standing Army: Fighting Climate
Change by Protecting Forests." *Nature Conservancy*, Vol. 58, No. 2, Summer 2008, p. 13.

Christenson, Anders, Roger Westerholm, and Jacob
Almén. "Measurement of Regulated and Unregulated
Exhaust Emissions from a Lawn Mower with and
without an Oxidizing Catalyst: A Comparison of Two
Different Fuels." *Environmental Science & Technology*, Vol. 35, No. 11, June 1, 2001, pp. 2166–2170.

Conservation International. "Saving Forests." Retrieved
August 8, 2008. http://www.conservation.org/learn
/forests/Pages/overview.aspx.

ConservationTools. "Economic Benefits of Biodiversity."
Retrieved September 25, 2017. http://
conservationtools.org/guides/95-economic
-benefits-of-biodiversity.

Diaz, Robert J., and Rutger Rosenberg. "Spreading
Dead Zones and Consequences for Marine Ecosystems." *Science*, Vol. 321, No. 5891, August 15,
2008, pp. 926–929.

Downie, Andrew. "Growth Potential." *Nature Conservancy*, Vol. 58, No. 2, Summer 2008, pp. 56–64.

Earth on the Edge. "How Much CO_2 Are You Emitting?"
August 2, 2015. http://www.earthontheedge.com
/how-much-CO_2-are-you-emitting.

Editors of E/The Environmental Magazine. *Green Living:
The E Magazine Handbook for Living Lightly on the
Earth.* New York, NY: Plume, 2005.

EPA. "Sources of Greenhouse Gas Emissions." April 14,
    2017. https://www.epa.gov/ghgemissions
    /sources-greenhouse-gas-emissions.
Goop. "Coming in 2017: A Ban on Microbeads."
    August 13, 2017. http://goop.com
    /coming-in-2017-a-ban-on-microbeads.
Greenpeace UK. "Forest Facts: 9 Things You Need to
    Know." July 27, 2017. https://www.greenpeace.org
    .uk/9-awesome-facts-about-forests-20140321.
Natural Resources Defense Council. "Issues: Global
    Warming." Retrieved August 3, 2008. http://www
    .nrdc.org/globalWarming/gsteps.asp.
Nature Conservancy. "Climate Change: What You Can
    Do." Retrieved July 9, 2008. http://www.nature.org.
NOAA's National Ocean Service. January 1, 2009.
    https://oceanservice.noaa.gov/facts/exploration.
Shah, Anup. "Biodiversity." Global Issues, June 14,
    2008. http://www.globalissues.org/EnvIssues
    /Biodiversity.asp.

INDEX

ABOUT THE AUTHORS

Nicholas Faulkner is a writer living in New Jersey.

Janey Levy is a writer and editor who has written numerous books for children and young adult readers. She lives on three acres near Colden, New York, in an energy-efficient log house that uses a geothermal system to heat the house in winter and cool it in summer. She recycles, uses compact fluorescent bulbs and environmentally friendly household cleaners, and takes reusable bags to the grocery store. She chooses energy-efficient appliances and makes gas mileage a priority when buying a car. Levy also contributes to the Nature Conservancy.

PHOTO CREDITS

Cover Klaus Vedfelt/DigitalVision/Getty Images; pp. 4–5 (background) namtipStudio/Shutterstock.com; p. 5 Gigira/Shutterstock.com; pp. 7, 14, 22, 30, 38, 46 pank2006/Shutterstock.com; p. 8 © iStockphoto.com/LeventKonuk; p. 10 Andrew F. Kazmierski/Shutterstock.com; p. 12 FenrisWolf/Shutterstock.com; p. 15 Wrangler/Shutterstock.com; p. 17 Win McNamee/Getty Images; p. 19 Emma Gibbs/Moment Open/Getty Images; p. 24 Tomasworks/Shutterstock .com; p. 27 © iStockphoto.com/JuliScalzi; p. 28 Andrew Aitchison/Corbis News /Getty Images; p. 31 Blew S/Shutterstock.com; p. 33 Brandon Alms/Shutterstock .com; p. 36 © iStockphoto.com/jfmdesign; p. 39 Kamomeen/Shutterstock.com; p. 42 Wavebreak Media/Thinkstock; p. 44 © iStockphoto.com/asiseeit; p. 48 rm /Shutterstock.com; p. 50 twildlife/iStock/Thinkstock; p. 52 Ramona Heim /Shutterstock.com.

Design: Michael Moy; Photo Research: Sherri Jackson